RADIO FREE QUEENS

RADIO FREE QUEENS

SUSAN MONTEZ

George Braziller
New York

First published in 1994 by George Braziller, Inc.
Copyright © 1994 by Susan Montez

All rights reserved
For information, please address the publisher:
George Braziller, Inc.
60 Madison Avenue
New York, NY 10010

Library of Congress Cataloging-in-Publication Data

Montez, Susan.
    Radio Free Queens / Susan Montez.
        p.   cm.
    ISBN 0-8076-1345-2
    I. Title.
PS3563.05425R34   1994
811'.54—dc20   93-39304
                                          CIP

Designed by Peter McKenzie

Printed in the United States of America
First Edition

Author's Note

I would like to thank my mother to whom
I am deeply indebted. She has always
supported my poetic endeavors with
absolute blind faith. I hope she doesn't
believe everything she reads.

Susan Montez
New York City, 1993

Acknowledgment is gratefully given to the following periodicals, in which some of the poems in this book originally appeared:

ARTFUL DODGE, "The Scale from Queens; or I Refuse a Large World"
ASYLUM, "To A. G."
CREAM CITY REVIEW, "Last Poem of the Season"
DUCKABUSH JOURNAL, "Gates of Jeddah"
GLENS FALLS REVIEW, "Road to Istina"
HAMPDEN-SYDNEY POETRY REVIEW, "War Memorial for Yugoslav
                                    Partisans"
LITTLE MAGAZINE, "Hardware"
LONG SHOT, "Inventory"; "Falling Rocks"
MARK, "More Talks about Hardware"
NEW YORK QUARTERLY, "Illinois Fantasy"
PANHANDLER, "Radio Free Queens"
PATCHWORK of DREAMS, "Buenos Aires Notebook"
PLASTIC TOWER, "Three Notes from Lajon"
POETRY EAST, "South Bronx I.S. 193 Social Studies Class Takes a Field
            Trip to Bronx Criminal Court"
PUERTO del SOL, "Meditations"
SOUTH COAST POETRY JOURNAL, "Aubade in Modified Second
                                    Asclepiadean"
13TH MOON, "The Travel Industry"
VOICES INTERNATIONAL, "Exercise"

To Binnie,
ma seule amie

CONTENTS

INVENTORY

In two weeks, I'm off for suntan, mineral
   baths, and communion with Indian gods.
   above cloudless horizon of desert skies.
   But, before departing, I want to say
   the following to you assholes who blew me
   off this year:
Fuck you, Felix, (Dante named names). You deadbeat—to ignore
   Citibank loan payments. Fuck you for not
   following me to Queens on winged feet to
   save marriage. Fuck you—hounding me about
   dominatrix past so I couldn't fly to Queens fast
   enough. What kink provoked me to tie up naked
   men and beat them, you say? Not sex, but
   rage. Sometimes I didn't beat them. I just tied
   them up, read aloud from the *Communist*
   Manifesto, accused them of corporate hooliganism,
   lectured on social diseases (saved lives),
   and condemned them for shabby family
   commitments.
Fuck you, Peter, sorry Kraut, less than heroic paramour. No
   balls! To run off to Palm Springs and schmooze among
   cactus, hobnob with desert flowers! Fuck
   you, you gave me the brush-off because I now
   work nine to five, got promoted, moved to Queens,
   lost panache—became ordinary. Another
   statistic, "Alone and divorced in Queens."
   Fuck you, you never knew the half of it.
   Never knew I was a whipmistress. Me, horrified
   you'd find out, be shocked, dump me. Or worse,
   want me to tie you up. Fuck your snooty
   comments about the R train. "How vill you
   manage on that old rattling train? Vat vill

you do alone in Qveens?"
Fuck you, Eric, seducing me at a Hollywood AA meeting
when I still had a husband, paramour, and less
than a year's sobriety. You, five years sober,
knew better than me, mesmerized by hot dry air and the LA
freeways' fast lights. Next morning, I caught a flight to
San Diego. Then you came to New York. Fuck
you, with your jet lag, you were a bore. Fuck
you for being appalled when you found out
I was once a dominatrix, then wanting me to tie
you up. I got $200 an hour to have my spiked
heal sucked and never took off a stitch.
After we finally made love, you got up and dialed
sports number, "Who won Mets game?" For once,
I didn't care. For once, I said, fuck you, Mookie.
Fuck you, Allen Ginsberg—snooty about MFA programs.
I adored you and you hurt my feelings. Made me feel
a schmuck for wanting to ride your cosmic
waves. Where but classroom would you give me
time of day? Fuck you for proposing marriage and
forgetting about it. I'm torn between calling
my lawyer for promise breached or calling
Page Six of the *Post*. Fuck you for not giving
attention I demand. I'll only yell louder.
Fuck you, Denise, my favorite pal at work. 10:00 A.M.
we'd listen to our daily horoscope. ("Hello,
Pisces.") But you transferred to another office.
Fuck you, Bob, appearing at my Lotto stand one rainy
day and proposing marriage when I haven't loved
you since 1979. Fuck your questions, too.
Fuck wanting me to tie you up.
Fuck everybody snooty.

Fuck everybody with an attitude about Queens.
Fuck everybody who wants to be tied up along flagpoles
    of Sixth Avenue.
Fuck everybody who thinks it's sad to live alone
    and divorced in Queens.
Fuck everybody who rejected me. You'll get yours.
    I'll name names.

MEDITATIONS

I do my thinking riding between
cars on the RR—Los accidentes
fatales más communes resultan
por caídas entre los wagones. Wean
off fear is my new directive. Hanging on
a chain, dazed with Walkman, I listen to
"Anytime, Anyplace, Anywhere."
You always hear me say this—doesn't dawn
on you it's a pop tune. But still true. Lights
illuminate mud-slushed tracks, a breeze, sub-
way trains, a good place to yearn. The rub
of wheel and rail! A flight
into darkness! I detrain, surface, Eighth Street,
half light of dusk, dim moon like wheat.

LITTLE VOICES

Cosmic waves in neighborhood zone around me.
Who is tapping? Continents miles off call for
answers. Morning, new launderette: between the

cycles wash or tumble dry, powers urge my
presence. Shaky double R pulls in station—
hot electric voices filter winter air—

Time for magic! Eye of the newt. Control of
meager life, pursuit of some hot tamales!
Come great thing—O lyrical roar, tin tongued gnu

blissfully present.

UNENDED CONCLUSIONS

For three years
we talked by phone,
some connections
better than others.
I had to imagine your end
from my office
or that phone booth on 47th Street
where I was yesterday,
the warmest day of winter.
We've come to agree
47th Street's the world's center,
a continental divide
mapped by diamonds,
commerce.
Every emotion needs a reference point
like physics and its $E=mc^2$.

Our equation,
the telephone wires'
two point distance
between here and there,
is unsolved.

WAR MEMORIAL FOR YUGOSLAV PARTISANS

At the monument, high in the mountains,
beyond Slano, you say,
"No schmoozen. Too disrespectful
with so many Czechoslovakians
paying homage to a system
that doesn't work."

At a metal mural depicting partisans facing
the enemy, I point out your people:
the ones aiming guns at women and children.

Back on the Balkan road, where daily,
cars ram the guard rail
and crash down into the Adriatic,
I imagine our death.

There could be worse fates than
dying together after visiting history.

Officials would dig out
passports from the rubble.
One dead German and a woman, born,
South Carolina. The guilty
always find each other.
And adulterers to boot.

But we drive on unharmed;
the monument, white and sun dazzled, behind us, along
with Nazis, Partisans, wives, husbands,
Hitler, and the Song of the South.

CANZONE FOR BINNIE

I.

When he returned from Rome,
He gave her the evil eye,
She said, and Richard's Aunt Rosa helped
To break the spell.

The angel sleeping sweet
He graciously gave to me
On Christmas. Spells, now, charms, love abounds
From cherub light.

She went to Catholic church,
Splashed holy water, lit candles,
Said a prayer to a patron saint.
The curse was off. Farewell.

II.

Eleven thirty-two
I finally call to say,
The eye is working still. Love has found
Its way to me.

She yells, "Say what?" My dreams
Of sweet Anthony, I tell,
We got engaged, in love, roses, vows,
An emerald ring.

"I can't abide it! Last night
Dreams echoed dreams!" she goes. "Frightful
Dream. I lost you in the subway, searched
The park, the zoo. Where? Gone!"

III.

"I found in bed the two
Of you. But the bed was turned
Around. You slept. He cursed, threatened,
eyed My holy eye!"

But why? To wound you? Dust
Your memory? I'm to fall
In love with him who loves you best, such
A vicious charm.

The magic books and runes used
past, amulets of warlocks, the
Virgin Mary, and the angel, St.
Theresa: Love-spell fly!

ILLINOIS FANTASY

I want sex with swans
while cameras roll, weeping
   willows waving lust
by a cool pond, floating pink
   flowers, lily pads to bathe and
fuck among—O pummeled black loam,
   in color, black & white, 16mm,
make me come with bird beaks
   and feathers, rapture me
on verdant prairies, taken by milkweed,
   thick strokes of milk oil
throbbing on eternity's canvas.
   Let grass grow under thighs
and the world vision plume fire.

AUBADE IN MODIFIED SECOND ASCLEPIADEAN

Cross out vodka and husband as
sunrise starts of the day. What to do? How to
think? Don't. Easy. I wear a Walk-
man tuned higher than loud. Disco for breakfast.

Wake up meaner when sober. Here—
grapefruit, cigarette lit. Hera, my muse, is
hot flame burning in oven.
Greek pal, Medea wakes. Chariots spin

black birds' skids on the kitchen floor,
0 Mount Olympus gods in Queens
seek out paradise soon. Coffee is blackest
hell, charred. Listen to me, or don't.

ROAD TO ISTINA

I wasn't always like this.
I was baptized—
a peaceful child dressed in white.
Waist-deep in holy water, I
sought comfort from the River
Jordan pastel-painted on the inside
of the baptismal pit.
In July heat, my soul was purged!

Now I purge with the gift of my ancestors—
Baptist preachers who screamed the gospel
from atop dead tree stumps.
My pulpit is this fire escape where
I stand this winter night, barefoot,
in the blackest hour.

Only I'm not talking to God.
I'm talking to you,
calling the police on me, three times,
for disturbing the peace.
Imagine, you'd have me arrested
after I took you into the night
to see the aurora borealis.

We slept among the pinecones,
woke with damp leaves. Then—
suddenly—you accused me of painting
the sky with vipers' blood and belonging
to an ancient Druidic cult which feasted
on evergreen needles and wine harvested
from deciduous leaves.

All I did was declare my love!

The law sirens peal,
summon me to the Tombs. I get one phone call,
so wait for the ringing just before dawn,
I'll tell you I love you
even if you don't want to hear it over
the wire or howled into the streets
during winter's gusty storm.

I'm purged, reborn by snow
red from the flashing light of patrol cars.
I'm ready to flee my pulpit,
having witnessed to you
and a sleeping city.

LAST POEM OF THE SEASON

Broken glass still on the linoleum;
sharp chunks, from last winter's tantrums,
heaped in piles
await the broom I never bought.
Now summer is over.
I'm accustomed to tweezing out
slices of blue, green, and ruby
from my heels.

I pull out paper and compile a list.
Summer events: affair with spy,
Tom Baker dies of heroin overdose—
proof there was this season
since I don't recall days growing longer.
But then, I set my clocks ahead,
so dusk never falls before midnight.

FALLING ROCKS

This is the way I read,
  "Forest Hills Rapist Strikes Again!"
  and think,
  he could come to Astoria, he could
  take the el or a taxi like anybody.
  Rape isn't what it used to be
  fuck psychological damage
  now you can get the Sida,
  I'll only say it in Spanish, Sida,
  and refuse the English.
And this is the way
  I dwell on that teeny bit
  of dope shot up 6 years ago
  trying to remember if we sterilized needles
  but think, "Hey, nobody's dead," then chant
  novinas, knock wood for weeks.
And this is the way
  if that rapist broke in, he'd have to shoot me
  because I'd be damned if I'd worry
  about Sida another 6 years.
Only this is the way I think
  worry is a sort of perpetual prayer to God
  so maybe I should just keep at it.
  Or maybe I should just fuck handgun laws
  and carry that .357 magnum
  my father gave me.
  I could blow a few heads off.
  Guns make me nervous
  so I don't keep it around,
  God only knows who I'd use it on,
  it wouldn't be protection
  all the time anyway,

what if someone snuck up behind
me on the subway platform? I'd
shoot them while falling
under the wheels of the F?
And this is the way I think
    I'm always surprised there
    aren't snipers on the subway.
    If I were a murdering psychopath
    I'd be a sniper and I'd snipe
    on the Brooklyn-bound F train at 5:30 P.M.
    going into the tunnel. And
    surely if I think these thoughts—don't
    others?
And this is the way I think
    good thing not too many people
    read poetry
    or I could be giving
    psychopaths ideas
    little censors come in and say,
    "Hey, watch what you write, you could
    be killing people."
And this is the way
    I figure even if you survived a gunshot
    wound or an oncoming train
    they'd ambulance you to the hospital,
    give a transfusion and
    boom, you've got the Sida.
And this is the way I think
    fuck these loans to Citibank
    and fuck Manufacturers too and Amex
    with their 18%—life is too short.
    I'll read that Dale Carnegie

How to Stop Worrying and Start Living book,
I'll have a nice life.
Maybe I could fall in love
like I did last summer with an almost
perfect guy, that divorced homocide detective
poet who slept with a Saturday
Night Special, lived in the neighborhood
and wanted to be a family man.
And this is the way
    I didn't worry about Sida
    but did worry he drank too much
    and might shoot me.
    It was a damn shame he wasn't sober
    with that gun, pension, and insurance
    plan—major medical, dental.
    We could've got married,
    become a nice Queens family,
    then retired to Florida.
And this is the way I think
    Ah, uh, uh, facades beware! He may look
    like husband material and a Mets fan
    but he's a drunk with a gun.
And this is just the way
    danger's everywhere.

LIFE AMONG THE ASHES

If this is a beach
on the Encantadas, then
the volcanoes are dead.
Better scorched by hot
lava than buried under
these cold ashes.

How did they get here, these ashes?
They came, one by one,
or in small groups,
blown in under the windows,
tracked in by strangers.
They conga'd down the chimney flue
until there were so many
I was trapped.

With a shovel I tried to burrow
my way out.
My arms tired, my eyes red,
I stopped.
As I rested,
my shovel turned to ash.

BINNIE AND I STOPPING ON A MOUNTAIN ROAD

On the mountain's blue peak, up a gravel
drive is "Monster Museum, Fortunes Read."
We can't pass it up though it has the dread
isolation of murder. A man sells
potions inside. High in these mountains, no
one will find us after this satanic
nerd sacrifices us in pedantic
ceremony. "He's odd, but harmless, so . . ."
So . . . only the mountains silent, puissant
have certainty, holding vast secrets next
to their rugged bosom. We may leave hexed—
"But we're closest to God." Cards read, I can't
wait to get out though our futures are charmed.
Going down dark mountains, I'm still alarmed.

EXERCISE

Clarity lit the confusion when
the train chose the ridge. Sharp,
bent soil and rocks plundered
the iron tracks driven across the

landscape. An effort to forgive
the margin. There will be no margin.
Draw out the desire from a broken
earth, choose to leave the bridge

exploded. It becomes less personal,
more symbolic. The symbol that
caused the motion, made things clear,
made confusion a river below.

vas a teen goddess
ong-legged
he Tudor house
ans and spots
edicine.
he spoiled daughter,
n school plays
ed on stardom in New York.

's in Dallas
o a millionaire.
a mansion,
dren and bad nerves.
s work half the time,
half, not.
sk is she'd lost
; after all,
ly one image
of anybody.

HARDWARE

New tools and the smell of nails
are a comfort
as if things can be accomplished by metal.
These duplicated keys, still oily,
are hard stuff made to fit
into a tight place and unlock
secrets with the precision
of their little teeth.
Little teeth biting at the facts,
she thought, and turned the latch.

Planted in a metal closet,
breathing the smells of rust and
his winter clothes,
she has a list of phone numbers
of unknown women.
The sounds of the bedroom
penetrate the door.
She can listen or wedge it open
to look if her eyes are made
of metal made to endure
the salts of the season.

MORE TALKS ABOUT HARDWARE

Kitchen cabinets are sprayed
white with automobile primer, and I've
learned to grease the joints of copper
tubing so the water runs down

from the faucet, drips, and erodes the porcelain,
while I dream waves driving
across oceans, driving me
with wishes to visit what's

already been built. Still, I watch
new door frames, panels
of Sheetrock taped neat with spackle.
Each pounding of a nail inflicts

a new order. It was me
who claimed the red banner
was a metaphor for freedom and adored
the parades of soldiers, ranked

in purpose. The purpose was hope
to build, to secure a nest with glued
twigs and live in peace. I wanted
to cut through this urge to wander with a sharp-

edged sickle and languish in
the domesticity for which the revolution
was waged. A bullet for a spoon! A cannon
for a pot! But the hammers and drills

sink into my eardrums, and I can't
love the building. I still cling
to historical disasters and yearn
to pick around the rubble of bombed-

THE TRAVEL INDUSTRY

We are each ships doomed to sink. *Titanics,*
Poseidons. We are planes destined not
to reach our destination. The old Aeroflot
office is gone. At my travel job, I pick
the topic: Anybody ever book
a death flight? Ooo, ooo. What a question!
But Glenn booked two on Eastern 401.
One survived, wanted a refund, then took
out bloody tickets My hands are clean. You
are safe with me. I dream places where planes
go down. Myriad voyages must rain
from past life experience. A thorough review
reveals out infinity. We are each ships
doomed to sink many times. Many crypts.

CHECK IN

Jets file the runway, rise up, heavy.
A man paces a platform. His hat,
suitcase and newspaper settle

next to him like pets. Flash,
a propeller clips a guide wire. A Piper
Cub explodes in the pines. The pines,

which warned against fog! Night
landings! The urgency to arrive! The
man shifts, checks his watch. We must

arrive by rail, the sky, the pitch
of open water. Trains speed by,
destinies tied to a rail. A leaf

breaks across the pavement. His
flight, boarding soon, validates
essential motion.

We go where we have to go,
while things crash, sink,
fall off cliffs.

ESCAPING THE PROPHETS

Don't question how it is when
I'm alone,
when I awake at the hour.
My purpose is to record
the coming of the slain lamb
or the scarlet beast.
Nights curled up cold
in the dirt of spirits,
angels in unknown color
saturate the room.
Will they flee if ignored
or pin me to the floor?
The stony buttress of the cemetery,
the tombstones assaulted!
I demand to know who lives there!
Who are you creatures so unsatisfied?
You nestled in the ground's sanctity.

TO CHICAGO

There is no music,
my lilac city, your gown
dropped to expose a naked bosom
when Frankie sang it all.

Yes, there were memories
like rain clinking in a rusted bucket.
Voices of emigrés rang on golf courses,
Picasso reproached industry.

Flat, square streets, fall brought parades
and cheerleaders. Too young to be a float princess,
I remember their ambitious pom-poms.
Land of tornadoes, unabashed reich
embossed on vellum paper

in some distant history.

JUNE

Surf City, East River, Astoria Park,
summer of sex plague '88.
Electrotelepathy zooms across bridge
from Harlem's hot pavement.
A city hot everywhere, hot and
unsatisfied awaiting miracle
of prodigal sins return. Blankets
and bodies sprawled in park,
clover, convertible Corvettes,
Cadillacs, speakers with disco
beat like sex objects—cruise by the river
racing cabin cruisers. O!
No thought of being ripped from urban woods
to rise up in purgatory,
and reborn in Sandusky! Death,
on such a temperate day
with soccer players among
trees green as moneyed
opulence is flatly
out of the question.

BUENOS AIRES NOTEBOOK

1) TRAVEL AGENT DIVERTIMENTO

Alone in Queens with horseradish
   divorced, roast beef for lunch,
I type: Dear John: I've had it
       with the glamour life,
       free travel, but no money,
       I quit, good-bye, Auf Wiedersehen,
       Sincerely, Agent 20.
Radio, "Quiero Rock," Mookie in left field,
   the fan whirs: "Don't quit yet. There's someone
to meet on the 7:05 Buenos Aires to Iguazu!"
   a flight booked last month, a connection
      for a client, not for me.

This client, Herr Baer, I'd had a crush on since processing his visa for Argentina. According to his visa form, he was perfect for me. Born in 1942, he was Swiss, divorced and living on Joralemon Street. I wanted to marry him and move to Brooklyn Heights, lounge with books, drink coffee at cafés midday.

No, that's not true. What I really wanted to do was stick Peter—throw another husband in his face—but bigger bargaining collateral this time.

   No more flights, no more flying
feet on the clouds. Ahh, but Argentina!
   Peróns, cafes, waterfalls, maybe
one last free ride before I'm wingless,
   grounded, a stone.
Drop off cat, bounce a few checks,
   tonight black sky, sapphire runway,
      Astoria lights below.

Actually, I don't go anywhere unless I have to. As Matthew Arnold once said

"There's not a damn thing out there." Of course, it was different with Peter.
Every three weeks I was on the 9 o'clock Lufthansa to Frankfurt or Pan Am
to Dubrovnik (with a change in Zurich and stop in Zagreb).

Now I stay around the neighborhood, go out to Shea on the weekend, maybe
to Brooklyn (not the Heights), or the Village.

2) BARADO/RETRASADO

Always the same. Now Buenos Aires,
    Aeroparque—across the road
the world's widest river, Rio de la Plata
    winter palm trees. Inside passengers
are piled at the gate, flight delays, fog, rain,
    low ceilings in Iguazu.

This is bullshit, and I can't believe what I'm doing—retracing Herr Baer's
itinerary. This Iguazu flight is where I thought the action was, but now the
only action seems to be delays. See, according to Herr Baer, I made a mess of
his South America trip. Liar, he messed it up himself by being an asshole
with the Brazilian authorities. But I took advantage of his claim (since we
hadn't met yet, and I was planning to marry him), called him up and said,
"So sorry, let me take you to lunch."

I took him to the Algonquin, the Rose Room. He looked just like his picture.
He also reminded me of Peter, or I pretended he did. Really I found his accent
obnoxious; whereas, I'd found Peter's German one charming.

2 weeks later, I wrote him a note.
    Dear Herr Baer:
    I've had a crush on you since October.
    I thought you'd ask me out when we had
    lunch. You should have, you'd like me.
    I'd fetch you trifles and never leave you
    at the mercy of wild beasts.

He ignored it. Paula said, "What'd you expect? He's Swiss. You should have written the note to his father asking permission."

Out 85 bucks for lunch (there's no price tag on love, but there is on fuck-ups), I thought, fuck Herr Baer, he's not my angel, my angel's on the flight to Iguazu.

Maybe the flight will be cancelled. Maybe
   I'll skip the jungle, Niagara would have been
closer anyway,

I used to book German tourists to Niagara every Saturday. That was when Peter was my client. At first, he was a dope, flirting, then bugging me about cheap fares for his groups to Miami—before we fell in love, before I knew he'd been living with Ushi, a cross-eyed girl in a fox coat, for 17 years (refusing to marry her), before he got tranferred, before I got married, before the day came when neither of us would be at 165 West 46th Street, me on the 9th floor, him on the 8th.

   but no—besides, there he is—
   jeans, white shirt, so young—
the one destined to this flight, the one
   I don't know, but will meet when
the fog lifts, wing flaps go down, rubber
   wheels bounce Iguazu runway.
I get up, go to the counter, order café solo.
   "No tengo cambio."
He follows. I look, he looks, nobody looks.
   I get out a book, if it were up to me
     all planes would be grounded.

I hate this flying around business. Travel restrictions, like communist countries had, are sensible. Loved ones stuck in Queens by order of the government, there's an idea. OK, I wouldn't have met Peter, but then, if I'd never met the love of my life—what would I be missing?

3) LAS CATARATAS DEL IGUAZU

We meet on the plane (always the same),
    32,000 feet, I hang
over his seat. He's going on to Saõ Paolo,
    making his change, but we exchange
names, numbers, Alberto. Alberto, citizen
    of Colombia but lives in Bethesda. We part
at passports like we should kiss, but don't.

*At Frankfurt Airport, Peter'd say, "We can't schmooze here—not with all
my colleagues around." But we schmoozed anyway. Serious schmooz. Holly-
wood. He must have been looking to get caught. The only place he ever refused
me (the last place we'd get caught) was at the War Memorial for Yugoslav
Partisans. It wasn't polite with all the Czechs paying homage to a system
that didn't work.*

I don't dawdle—a rush to go
    nowhere. Damp green jungle,
taxis, tour buses, guides with whistles,
    "Over here, please. People, people!"
outside the glass terminal.

*Peter started in the travel business as a guide in Constanta, Romania. Except
for 7 years in New York, he was always getting assigned to countries "under
the pressure." He'd call from Yugoslavia and say, "It's hot here, and the
communists are bugging me."*

    Grab a cab.
"¿Adónde?" he says. I
should have stayed on the damn plane,
    my visa's good, travel agent trails
stranger through South American skies.
    That's the glamour life—how to explain jet

set whimsy without seeming an ax murderer? I stay
    with plans: Foz do Iguazu, Las Cataratas,
solarium boat under the Falls.

Actually Alberto invited me to Bahia, his final destination. Frankly, I
thought he was kidding. Had I known he was serious, would I have gone?
No, my luggage was in Buenos Aires. Besides, Alberto and I would see each
other again. That was part of the Herr Baer plan—that I should seek out
an old Swiss coot and end up with a South American child.

4) ARGENTINA TE QUIERO

Alone in Buenos Aires con Coca-Cola,
    café solo, a confiteria on the corner
Entre Rios and Belgrano. Why here? Argentina?
    Solamente. A family town, padres y madres,
teenagers smoking. Me—no familia no niños,
    mi ex-esposo, I read here in NY paper,
is in a big play. Paula once said, "Imagine
    if he gets rich and famous and
you've left him." Across the street a sign,
    "Argentina Te Quiero," New York Te Quiero,
      not the same, I walk
    "Together Forever" blasting from
Avenida de Florida record stores. I think of
    strangers, the one I married,
the one on the 7:05 Buenos Aires to Iguazu.

I could end up alone the rest of my life on foreign continents. I haven't even
seen Peter for 15 months. Maybe it's time to take action into my own hands.
I'll improve my German, fly to Frankfurt, rent a car, drive to Eschenburg—
have a talk with his mother. Mothers can never resist women truly in love
with their sons.

5) UPPER DITMARS BOULEVARD

In Queens, always the same, I hear
   the el cascade into Ditmars Station.
No Alberto, no horseradish,
   safe on the couch, I type:
      Dear Alberto: I've had a crush
      on you since Iguazu.
      Let's meet, you'll like me.
      I'll fetch you wild beasts
      and never leave you
      at the mercy of trifles.
   My checks bounce all
over town. I see on the news:
Queens woman axed to pieces in vacant
   lot (not my neighborhood) and a plane
crash in Argentina.

6) BLACK CLOUDS

30 nights from Iguazu, Alberto calls,
   just back from Brazil when
New York is steaming, airless, Queens beaches
   closed from medical waste and sewage.
"Come down this weekend," but I have no tan,
   no clothes, no flash, but he's leaving
for Europe next week!

*He's going backpacking! Staying at youth hostels! Oy vey—just how young
is he? 19—I'm 32, Peter's 46, 14 points one way, 13 the other. Whenever I
asked Peter to run off with me, his standard answer was, "Yes, and in 5
years you'll dump me for some young guy."*

Airplanes! Jet fumes!
   Landing lights! Don't fly off again,
damn it—stay in Bethesda, a shuttle flight
   away, every half hour on the hour
and the half hour—more frequent than the
   GG Brooklyn Queens Crosstown.
But he's all I've thought about—
   destiny's long approach.
On Friday, I'm at the airport—
   6:30 shuttle, departed, on time, 7:30
on time, an electrical storm approaches,
   but they say we'll make it out.

7) DOVER BEACH

Alone con Alberto, black trees, night,
   "I wanted to follow you," I say,
"Why didn't you?" he says. I say, "You can't
   follow someone on a whim."
"Why not?" he says.

*At 19, you can do anything you want. Why not 32? Why not 46? Who makes
these rules? Germans, that's who!*

   Brazil, Argentina,
   New York City, Maryland loam!
Finally we kiss among tree bark mosquitos. Let's stay!
   Make the airplanes go away!
Hide in the house, lock doors,
   chain ourselves to the radiators,
renounce the world! Nothing—
   only runway after runway,
dim lights from dimmer cities.

Alberto's too young to know the radiator game, and I won't teach it to him even though I went down with that idea, thinking it was the only game we had to play. But modern houses in Bethesda don't have radiators. He wouldn't want to learn it anyway.

8) NO IDEAS BUT IN THINGS

Alone in Bethesda, alone with Alberto's
    blue quilt, Heineken can pencil
holder, German desk lamp, photos (Alberto
    sailing off Brazil coast, who this?

Girlfriend?), bookcase without many
    books—school texts, economics, sports
trophies, medals, Walt Whitman High School
    yearbook,

Alberto's in his brother's room (the family's in Colombia). We didn't exactly have a fight—nothing got that far. It's OK, I can be Zen about it, besides, I'm fascinated by his possessions. This is his life, this is how he lives, and it has nothing to do with me.

      clothes in closet taunt me,
"We're busy—who let you in here anyway?
    Go back to Queens." I couldn't
agree more.

Alberto's life is not a life I should be interrupting, one way or the other, good or bad. Peter's, on the other hand, I should be interrupting, good or bad. His life is my life.

Peter's a coward and wants to do nothing but wait, like waiting in some hateful Beckett play. That's it, I'm going to march right into Frankfurt with heavy artillery and turn the place to rubble, (Peter remembers when it was

really rubble, he always said, "Frankfurt and I grew up together.") —hold
him prisoner, then offer up the Marshall Plan.

    Desire splinters
  into lawns, malls, cheerful cars,
DC discoteques, VCRs and unused
    Nonoxynol condoms.

So that's what broke Peter and me up—a dose of chlamydia. And where did
it come from? Peter said he didn't have it, but that's impossible! If I had it,
he had it—there was no one else! I asked my doctor about this, I said, "Leon,
what gives?" He said, "Maybe you really didn't have it. Maybe the lab made
a mistake. Maybe it was yeast." But I blamed Peter, and he blamed me.

9) BLAME IT ON RIO

Who good-looking stranger driving
  me across Potomac, what state now?
Maryland, Virginia? What country, jungle, city
  airport, Korean fruit stand, Brooklyn
Manhattan transit stop underground or el in
  Mass Transit of life? "Face it,"
Alberto says, "We made a mistake."

"Face it," Peter said, "we made a mistake—thinking we could do this with
so many miles between us." I got hysterical, made a jerk of myself, bawling
and beating my head against a Steigenberger airport sign.

    I don't make mistakes! Not sitting
alone in Queens with horseradish, quitting
  job, ball game watch, Mookie at plate,
when cosmic wave jettisons across electric
  el rail across rooftops—Lefkos Pirgos,
2 family houses, P.S. 85 into my window
  with message—GO TO IGUAZU—THERE'S SOMETHING

THERE! No! No mistake! But maybe
   a misdirection, a failure to
read the fine print. I say, "Blame it on Rio,"
   as we pull to the curb.

*Alberto drove me to National in his mother's car, some sort of Japanese job.
I felt like crying but wasn't sure why. Disappointed, he said he'd wanted
things to work out splendidly (yea, yea, and I wanted to marry Herr Baer,
move to Brooklyn Heights). I kissed him good-bye on the cheek then thought,
"What trouble that would have been."*

A FINE HOUR

Once, enamored of an actor
who ate fire between acts of *Hamlet*,
I sat amidst the torch lights of the
outdoor stage. I let the porcelain

planets pass, not thinking of their
rings or spots in the inky well
of night. I was searching for the

elusive arc, the duration of a moment.
Forged-iron sculptor, fire-eater, I
counted on the glow to last. But flames
were extinguished when swallowed.

ORPHAN SONG

Come little orphans to the meadow
Come little orphans all be found
Motherless waifs half dressed and dirty
Come to the fount and all be crowned

Come little orphans don't be lonely
Angels and elves wait at the gate
Evil spirits have all been buried
Hurry now it's getting late

Don't distress in darkened alleys
Don't cry out in thund'rous skies
There's a place of peace no worry
Light above the night does rise

Come little orphans bells are ringing
From the steeples in the vales
Lilies and rainbows are awaiting
Just beyond the fact'ry dales.

GATES OF JEDDAH

Walk with me to the gates of Jeddah
and see the world I've created from bits
of lilacs and pearls found in an old Arab
trunk. How long I've waited to be here;
forging deserts against the sands' currents
and crossing seas where the salt beat
my spirit. Now you must come with me
for a feast of vine leaves skewered over
lamb prepared by Moslems under mosques.
We shall begin what forty centuries have
destined from the broken pieces of antiquity
that lie before us on these sands.

Walk with me to the gates of Jeddah
and see the world created from the smoke
of Brooklyn and concrete hunks stored in a bottle.
Swim with me by the reef and take the children
for tea at the market where old men smoke
pipes under slanted roofs. We shall sit
on the day of rest, map our future across one
hundred continents until we are feeble—
ready to perish.

CLASSICS

I thought I was Medea
when I pushed her down the stairs,
and some king or god
owing me a favor would say,
"Jump into this chariot drawn by dragons
and be ferried safely back
to the land of sand and pine trees
you call home."
Instead, I stood at the top of the stairs
looking guilty as a Gypsy
concealing a strangled chicken
and said,
"Hey man, she fell."
I don't deny smirking
at the blood-soaked dress,
and the blood which matted her gold hair.
I thought I smelled smoke
of dragons flaming through the hall,
flying to my rescue.
But it was only smoke from apartment
fourteen bathed in gasoline.
"Let those blue flames devour," I shouted
"unfaithfulness and consume—"
Is it true?
Men only love Greek women
and cast out all that's foreign?

STRANGE DICTIONARY WORDS

A windpipe severed
senseless where the
shade tree over-
extended fatigue.
Metric miasma! The
metropolis kissed
bugs of knavish
need; the kinky
kinnikinnink of
kinsfolk. Emergency!
Internal mysteries.
Constrain beneath the
gauge of night owls.
Help!

DARREL,
OUR MESSENGER

sent orchid bouquets, African violets,
Balsam of Mecca bath oils to Karen
for two weeks, then proposed. His tourmaline
gifts got him a kiss one night, streets wet
from rain and dew—then it all fell apart—
like his old Bronx gang, the Black Spades, marauders
on empty el trains. We'd asked, "Did you mur-
der? Slash, steal?" Karen refused him, a tart
no. She knew he moonlit as a stripper
(maybe gave blowjobs!), went to beach parties in
basements where women pranced naked like violins
of sex. He fucked them with fruit, wove their fur,
and licked the tropical juices. Laissez-faire
mornings he woke in strange underwear.

Darrel missed work a week so Karen called
him (she missed his gifts), he pleaded Bronx nights, no
need for jobs, besides he'd been in jail. Oboe
music was playing and Karen said, appalled,
"You better be careful, especially these
days." He said, "That's the way I am." I said,
"You slept with him?" She said, "No way," set dead
against it. Manhattan blooms burst from trees,
spring hats, colors. Darrel, in his dark bed,
now drenched in watermelon rinds, had seeds
stuck to his groin. Who'd been there? All roads lead
to a plummet in the vat. Karen filed
her nails, spritzed perfume. He never came back
Karen said, "This new hair spray's like shellac."

DOLORES

A nude woman in a brass bath
dries off. Powder perfumes a path
of diamonds and stars.
Her hair is twilight, sleek tar,
in a loose French braid.
She's a fantasy—a commercial.
She's the woman not pulling
the ox cart. She is not
the ox. She is loved, apart,
but only a vision, the undiseased
nude of capricious dreams unseized.

THE SCALE FROM QUEENS; OR, I REFUSE A LARGE WORLD

> Confucius: The planet
> shrinks like cotton in a hot
> dryer.

O Caribé! Island Music, wet air and steel drums!
I fall in love (or something
like it) with a Lebanese med student from Beirut
by way of Toledo. 1,680 miles: Virgin Islands
to Astoria. 517 miles: Lake Erie to East River.
"Meet me," I telegram, "first toll plaza
on Ohio Turnpike from Indiana
where during tornado season I visit
the grassy banks of St. Joseph River."
A quick drive. But not quick enough!
Where is my low orbit plane? When will Pluto
move closer to Mars? And Queens to Asia? Alas!
I drink coffee, draw random destinations
with specific meaning—a Lebanese from
Land of Headlines found in Caribbean—and me
awestruck in tropical disco with green lights
and reggae band dreaming turnpikes, marriage,
civil war.

IN A RUT

Angels appear to him in the pool room.
Halos burn through smoke.
"Why do you live in this purgatory?" they ask,
as a solid ball plunks in the corner pocket.

Drafts on the table, burning filters in the ashtrays,
old men eye the angels. Not locals,
they think, and ask the time.
There was a time he was much younger, but he
is still with the young. His circle of blond flatterers
follow his small successes, play the jukebox,
and take turns sharing his bed.
"We are grieved," the angels moan, "to see
the jackals hunt the jackals.
You had a vision but are prepared
to let it die in the fold of flesh and stale beer."
"Speak English," he growls and takes a swing
at the divine creatures with his cue.

EASTER POEM

Supreme divine—ecstasy gives

a saint like Theresa, sublime
   when pierced by holy arrows tipped
   in Godly seed and nectar dipped
by seraphs garbed in gold. O time

of God and angel bliss—lift up
   my skirt to holiness, insert
   the wand! O Jesus, shower spurts
of paradise to harp and cup

and dust and Hell—lie down upon
   my mortal breast and reap the flesh
   of thigh, pink blossom flower. The mesh
of scepter, rod and loin undone

upon the satin sheets. O love
   O bliss O happiness to feel
   your spirit up inside now seals
my fate beside the fleeting dove.

TO EX-DOMINATRIXES

1)
Oh little mistresses,
   Wo ist du now?
   Chased away
   to boutiques, husbands,
   fluorescent offices,
   pumping gas &
   waiting tables,
      your latex & leather & spikes
         junked in attics,
         basements,
         atop trash.

2)
First, you weren't whores
   strewing toe flowers
   in the mouths of foot fetishists.

First, you weren't whores
   but moon queens who
   prodded gagged men
   with electric charge.

First, you weren't whores
   but maybe rip-off artists
   listening to dull businessmen
   fantasies.
   You tied them up,
   did nothing,
   left them strung, alone,
   to go smoke cigarettes & play Galaga.

Some accused: "You're dishonest!

I paid for this fantasy
but was only bound, abandoned!"

As if money meant entitlement.
As if you were whores.
As if honesty was truth's compromise.

3)
They'd drop to their knees,
   Corporate board rooms!
   Copy centers!
   27th floor cafeterias!
They'd kneel,
   worship,
      think you're a whore
   be pissed on, kicked,
      think you're a whore
   rubber sodomized,
      whore

But you were Mistress! Goddess! Superior Divine!

ORACLE

39th and Beebe el platform— I await the GG
   which doesn't run on this track, except today I think it
will. I wait, wait but no train, finally I ask the token
   clerk. "Yes, yes," in an accent, "the GG will come here,
but not for a while. Besides when it comes, it'll wait 20
   minutes for all passengers." I take a walk, find Binnie
and Bob smoking under the el, convince them to come for
   lunch at the frontier where a wall separates Queens
from Brooklyn. It's a new wall, I don't know where it came from, we
   find a tar-paper joint with grimy windows under the el.
Is Brooklyn now communist? They say they don't think so but
   aren't sure, but anyway, no one needs visas anymore
to go anywhere. We have goulash, and I worry
   about missing the train. Outside there's smoke and fog and all
planes are grounded. I want to know where the planes are, no one'
   clear on that point. It could be fog, but no, they think the planes
are gone for good. "There'll be some boats," Bob says, "but only slow
   ones, and some trains." "Good," I say, "good, no more of this insane
flying around, no more jet fumes of separation." I
   can't convince them to take the GG to the end of
the line. They leave, disappear, go to Manhattan. The sun
   comes out, bright, and I have no sunglasses. Finally it comes,
the GG, the Brooklyn Queens Crosstown, everyone's crammed inside.
   Everyone's European, they think I'm a tourist,
I think I'm a tourist too. So when they ask where I'm going,
   I say, "To the end of the line, for the adventure." The men
are wearing green felt hats with feathers, like Austrians, and
   claim they don't usually take the GG. No, no, they take the
F from Forest Hills. But today things are fucked up, trains are
   on the wrong tracks. They'll make other connections
in a few stops. "You should change too," they continue. "The GG
   becomes dangerous. Maybe you'll get all the way okay,

but maybe not. Pointless to die for a stupid trip." They're
    right, in theory. Disappointed, I get off the next stop,
how will I know what the GG's like? Is it elevated?
    Or underground? Is it really dangerous? What's at the end
of the line? I catch a bus—open-sided with a striped
    canopy. Glenn's on the bus, he's touring America.
"Are you touring America?" he asks. I'm not sure.
    The bus stops at the board house. "What's a board house?" I ask.
"It's the board house, you know," Glenn says, but I don't know.
    I sit on the board house porch and watch people go in, sign lists,
take brochures and arrange things, like in a visitor's center.
    There are bus tours, opera tours, and group tours of the GG.
I'm told I'm in Astoria but don't recognize the oak trees. Which side
    of the el, East or West, am I on, I wonder.

THE TREE OF PARADISE

You said your feet had walked
the swamps and deserts
of one hundred countries.
My quick feet tracked you
to an obscure island rumored
to be the original Garden of Eden.
The tree was on the southern tip
of this paradise, near an oil field,
where no one wanted to go.
But we went.
You fell climbing the limbs
of ancient wisdom.
I drove you around
the hospital in a wheelchair,
your leg in a cast.
I would have married a gimp,
but you took yourself out of Eden
to a real hospital (out of the Salmanaya
where you accused doctors of infecting
cracked bones).
Except too late. The leg must go.
Now only one tired foot to explore
the world.

TO A. G.

Irritation festers inside a sock.
Shoes off, I walk around in it
awhile as distant ceilings
open to more inviting heavens.

Who needs popes to figure
out details? Tea doesn't walk
from the kitchen. The cat doesn't
fetch, pisses outside the litter

box. My hands are dried from Lysol
and truth is on the clothesline
flapping in the breeze. The clocks
tick and resist trials. Look,

a bulldozer through tasseled corn.

NEW AND VARIED LANDS

Phoenicians started it
   cruising the Mediterranean using
      merchandising" as their excuse.
Or maybe it was that old fool Noah
   with his ark—screaming at the wife,
      the kids, animal pairs,
         We've got to go! The flood's coming!"
There was no flood, he made it up—
They should have stayed home
   there was no place to go.

Or, take Marco Polo sailing to the Orient
for silk—not even dry cleaning back then—
   and he wants silk.
   He could give a shit about silk,
   he wanted to go out on the ship,
   sail out from the harbor,
   battle tidal waves,
   risk lives, watch
   swabbies slapped by the boom
   into oceanic despair
   then gobbled by sharks.

Fuck him, Fuck Magellan, Fuck Marquette,
   Fuck Columbus—with their
   selfish gallivanting.
They should have stayed home,
   there was no place to go.

But the Wright brothers really turned the tide
   right there on Hatteras
   the scene of shipwrecked thousands
   with their airplane invention.

Why didn't they stick with bicycles?
　A good invention
　from home to village, village to home,
　What else do you need?

But no—they've to get everybody airborne
　propellers, jets, helicopters,
F-16s, People Express, Frank Lorenzo,
special meals and no smoking aisle seats.

Old ladies, punks, businessmen,
poets, mobsters all rushing the 9 A.M. to Chicago,
night flights to Europe, Rio, or Burma
　even back to Phoenicia

like there's someplace to go.

Rushing off with cameras, briefcases,
phony passports, European adapters,
cordless irons, folding toothbrushes

Let them go—let
all of them go by ship, plane,
　or Hovercraft
　Let them all leave everything behind.

BURIED LIVES

No respect to time or distance! Scanners
find me! You, who swore you'd never
leave, but left, persist
in acting as vigil with claims
you leave your body, let your spirit
float around the earth.

Your body did seem old, as though
yours from another life. Maybe
you returned, plucked it from the graveyard
and use it now.
It's comfortable.

I sit on the F train
and read the *Post*.
Rush hour, among Lower East Side
Chassids, Park Slope executives,
I think of my latest romance—
a nice man who takes me to dinner,
wants to share a thought,
a feeling.

You once said,
perched on a wall by the Hudson,
"I condemn the little romances, pregnant
with kisses and sour commitments.
I hate the marriages born,

bearing boredom and infidelity.
All of it means nothing,
nothing
because it's not eternal!"

In the evening, I sit wrapped

in smoke and pearls. Witch ointment
wards you off, but I know
you're in the restaurant, invisible,
at a better table, where the candle blinks
Morse code. Rich wax cries from the wick.

My date thinks I own the lock
of ancient wisdom. From my eyes,
he senses secrets.

But they are not my secrets!

Furious that he mistakes me for
the spirit who hounds me, I spill
wine and shriek, "Ancient
wisdom blinds me. I can't help
the buried lives. I don't want to know
what I wasn't meant to know! What
was forgotten! Vive la Communisme!"

He leaves, believes I'm an animal.
Nuts. You are content
having cleaned the static between
receiver and transmitter.

My Virgil, committing yourself
to reminders of that other time.

SOUTH BRONX I.S. 193 SOCIAL STUDIES CLASS TAKES A
FIELD TRIP TO BRONX CRIMINAL COURT

Still sipping coffee and in a bad mood, I confiscate a Tootsie Pop
    from Doreen. She whines, "Oh give it back, Teacher, oh please."
But I won't. Word's gotten out that I'm soft, I dump the sucker.
    A November day: yellow leaves float down and drown in the damp
street, black smoke pours out an apartment chimney. Surely, there's
    a law against such smoke mushrooming around the school mingling
with the leaves, making them dance, yet here it is, the Second Circle.
    The kids complain about the school bus. They want to take the
train, afraid of being mistaken for special ed. kids or retarded
    ones. But we get on, roll through the smoke, through the half-
dressed trees of Crotona Park and block after block of burnt-out
    buildings. I could take a picture, "Look, here's Dresden."
It wouldn't be questioned. These charred hulls are majestic with
    their mosaics, granite bodies, and blackened eyes. A few are
still intact painted fresh with boxes of begonias and slum geraniums.
    A daring statement. The class has gotten rowdy by the time
we park on the Grand Concourse, yelling out the window, "Hey, you're
    ugly!", and bouncing on their seats to see who can hit their
head the hardest on the bus roof. "Ouch!" Jaimie squeals. "Jaimie,"
    I ask. ¿Tú estás estúbido hoy?" The school drug counselor tries
to quiet them down but has no success. "Shut up," I demand, "or this
    bus goes back to school." I've been threatening to cancel
the field trip all week even though it's an anti-drug program. Last
    week we went to Bronx Lebanon Hospital to see "how drugs make
people sick." Our guide pointed out Thumbelina babies in oxygen tanks
    hooked up to wires and tubes saying, "These babies are sick
because of drugs." Sick with what, she did not mention. Today, we
    are here for a drug trial. I get my flock to the 7th floor and
remind Lindale I have parental permission to tape his mouth.
    Even with Lindale quiet, the courtroom's incredibly noisy—

airplanes and sirens unceasingly roar and rattle the windows. The
    judge talks about being a judge and judging drug cases.
"How much do you make?" Javier asks. "100,000 a year. Maybe stay
    away from drugs, you can have my job." Still, the trial is
boring, the courtroom warm, and I get sleepy. The defendant is accused
    of selling 20 glasines of heroin to an undercover officer.
The money in the evidence bag is not the money designated for the
    buy-and-bust deal. That's the key, the defense argument.
I'm about to doze when I hear, "Teacher, please approach the bench."
    Shit, I think, slinking by the heroin dealer, assistant D.A.,
court stenographer, and cute detective (6th precinct, formally Bronx
    narcotics) to hear, "Ms. Montez, your class is getting fidgety,
maybe they've had enough." I couldn't agree more, but the school
    drug counselor intervenes. The bus won't arrive for another
forty minutes, couldn't we please stay. He promises the class will
    be good. Your promise, not mine, I remind him, and go back to my
seat to snooze. Still, we have to leave before the verdict.
    You know he's guilty but will beat the rap on that technicality.

THREE NOTES FROM LAJON

Dear Renita,
You are mad at Francisco
Yes or no. Draw a check next to it.
Because I no Francisco.

Dear Brad Did you say that you like me
yes or no check one of them OK because
I like you OK. And you are very cute
and you no you are too and everyday
I see you you say hi and walk away

Dear Francisco,
Did you talk to Brad yes or no.
Renita is mad because Shantel
wrote that letter. Did you right
her back yes or no. Please talk
to Brad.

RADIO FREE QUEENS

Poetry's a ham radio
   broadcasting to those
      misplaced in 50 states.

If I were rich,
   I'd hire a detective,
      "Go find Corky Martin,

here's money, make phone calls,
   fly first class, do what
      you gotta do, just find

him, last seen, 1964, red hair,
   black glasses, black
      turtleneck, skateboarding

with brother, Tim. Find Tim,
   his sister Anne, his father,
      once a doctor, Elkhart, Indiana.

I heard they moved,
   St. Louis, California, back to
      Greenwich, the way

Americans go—
   If people stayed put,
      who'd need you

tracing 18-wheel moving vans?
   Who'd be victim
      to Red Ball, Allied,

airplanes, statio wagons,
   address books lost
      in transit?"

We met after the Palm
  Sunday tornado,
    the same week President

Johnson declared Elkhart
  a disaster area,
    and parted the same

autumn when green leaves
  and willows wearied
    into reds and browns.

Last year, I thought I saw him
  on 6th Avenue, in front
    of 1212, a passing

oracle, his red hair ebbed
  into Chassid crowds, past
    Simpson's red neon

diamond displays. I walked up
  6th, delirious, the Exxon fountain
    weeping, funnel clouds

steaming from subway grates.
  Love should boomerang back,
    circle round

like the Ferris wheel we were stuck
  on at the Goshen County Fair
    when Corky won me

a stuffed snake. O bliss—
  stranded high on
    mechanical wheel

forever. Last night, a dream:
Corky found by accident
in a Greenwich Village jazz

club. His hair, shorter,
less red, but still Corky,
grown up, the smell of prairie

musk remembered from a pink
comb used through his hair,
ambrosia I carried

across 14 states in the back seat
of my parents' Coupe de Ville.
He was in New York,

dream business, but lived
in Houston. I thought I'd have
to chase him, send clever notes,

trifles, nosegays, Persian cats,
but he declared love among
the jazz club saxophones.

Then I awoke
to the sun, alarms
of Astoria, a plane roaring

overhead to La Guardia.
I got a cigarette,
dialed Houston directory,

"The number for Martin,
first name, Edmund."
A recording:

"I'm sorry, at the customer's
    request, that number
        is not listed."

But still, an Edmund
    Martin in Houston. Could it be?
        Corky revealed in a dream?

Corky driving a Toyota on Katy Freeway,
    working in Galleria offices,
        landing at Hobby?

What money, what miracles
    to find him?
        And if found

would he think me a kook?
    Refuse me, have a wife,
        kids, judge me

a marauder, une femme malade
    dangerous sort
        in tabloids obsessed

with guns and gasoline cans?
    No grip. Stuffed
        snakes, Persian cats,

if anyone knows
    the whereabouts of Edmund
        "Corky" Martin,

contact Susan Montez,   ·
    Astoria, Queens,
        reward offered.

SUSAN MONTEZ was born in Virginia and educated at Columbia University and Brooklyn College. She is presently a full–time instructor of English composition at Norwalk Community–Technical College. Her work has appeared in many literary journals such as *Poetry East, New York Quarterly, Asylum* and others. *Radio Free Queens* is her first book of poetry.